This book was made possible through a generous gift from an anonymous family.

This book belongs to:

_____

Prager University ("PragerU") is the world's leading educational nonprofit focused on changing minds through the creative use of digital media. Taking full advantage of today's technology and social media, we educate millions of Americans and young people about the values that make America great.

Our K-12th grade educational initiative is working to restore traditional American values in elementary, middle, and high schools across our great nation. With entertaining and educational videos for students of all ages, special curated pro-America resources, and an online community of freedom-loving parents and educators, PragerU gives you the tools and resources to provide students with a healthy and balanced education. To learn more, visit PragerU.com/Kids.

All Text and Illustrations Copyright © 2021 Prager University Foundation.

All rights reserved, including the right of reproduction in whole or in part in any form.

PragerU is a registered trademark of Prager University Foundation.

Published by PragerU

15021 Ventura Boulevard #552

Sherman Oaks, CA 91403

Today Is Christmas

PragerU

Ruff Ruff! I'm Otto. It's almost **Christmas**! In homes all across America, Christmas trees are covered in ornaments and twinkling lights. Families come together to celebrate. But first, it's time for another big adventure.

My best friend, Dennis, climbed into his father's big, red, leather chair. "This is our sled," he said.

"Can it be our time machine?" I asked.

"Yes, Otto. We can use it to go back in time and learn about Christmas."

"Ho! Ho! Ho!" I barked. "Here we go!"

ZOOM... We flew in our sled to the first Christmas night.

"Weeee! This is fun, be sure to hold on tight!"

We arrived in a place known as the **Holy Land**.

"A special location," said Dennis as I reached for his hand.

A big, bright light lit up the midnight sky.

"It looks like a star," I said, pointing up high.

We came upon **three wise men** who appeared to be kings.

Gold, frankincense, and myrrh they carried, along with other things.

They introduced themselves as Melchior, Gaspar, and Balthazar.

Long had they traveled, following that big, bright star.

Together we walked as far as our feet were able,
'til we came upon a young family resting in a stable.

"Who's that?" I asked, pointing at a newborn baby boy.

Gaspar said, "We believe he's our Savior; his birth fills us with joy."

Melchior said, "We followed that star up in the sky so bright;

it led us to a baby called **Jesus** on this first Christmas night."

Dennis said, "Thank you for teaching us about this special day.

We've learned so much, but we must be on our way."

We said goodbye and exchanged some pleasantries.

Then ZOOM... flew forward a full three centuries.

We saw a man there, walking on the street.

He looked like a bishop, with a robe down to his feet.

He grinned to himself as down the street he strolled.

Into an open window, he tossed a bag of gold.

The bag landed in stockings hung by the fire.

His generosity was truly a thing to admire.

He said, "I'm helping the poor by giving them gifts.

That's why I came to be known as **Saint Nicholas**."

"Saint Nick," I asked, "are the stories about you true?"

He replied, "Some say they're legends, but I'll share them with you."

"I created the stocking stuffer," he said with a smile.

Dennis added: "That tradition has lasted all this long while."

We bade him goodbye, got into our sled, and off we flew...

We **ZOOMED**... forward through time to 1962.

We landed at the White House and saw a big Christmas tree.

"Otto, there's the president, **John F. Kennedy**."

"Daddy!" shouted two small children, and into the room they raced.

They ran to the president and wrapped their arms around his waist.

"Mr. President," we said. "How do you do?"

"We're Dennis and Otto. It's an honor to meet you."

"Welcome to the White House," said JFK.

"We're getting ready for Christmas, a very special day."

Dennis said, "We're traveling through time to learn about the Christmas season."

"It seems important," I said. "Can you tell us the reason?"

The children's response was instant: "We get gifts and sweets! There's popcorn and candy canes and lots of other treats!"

"Presents are nice," their father agreed, "but there's more to this day. It's a special time for families to gather, worship, and pray."

Said his wife **Jackie**, entering gracefully through the open door,

"We must also remember, this time of year, to give to the poor."

"I love the Christmas season," said Dennis, "and I'm a Jew."

"Really?" I asked. "So, the phrase 'Merry Christmas' doesn't exclude you?"

"Not at all," said Dennis. "I say it frequently — in fact, all the time!

What's more, another Jew — **Irving Berlin** — composed 'White Christmas' and even made it rhyme."

I asked, "Is it only Christians who celebrate this day?"

"Christmas is a national holiday for all Americans," answered JFK.

Dennis said, "Boy, is that ever true!

So, let me say 'A very Merry Christmas' to all of you."

"Thank you, Mr. President," said Dennis.

"You've made this evening so bright."

Again, Merry Christmas to all, and to all a good night!"

Then we got into our sled and ZOOM...
"Ho! Ho! Ho! Off we go!" and back to Dennis's room.

"That was my favorite adventure yet!" I barked.

"You say that every time, Otto."

"Well, I loved learning about Christmas."

"It is an incredible story," said Dennis, "going back 2,000 years from the Holy Land to almost every country in the world."

"Plus, all those presents and tasty treats!"

"That's true, Otto, but more importantly, Christmas is about faith, family, and charity."

"You mean giving to other people?" I asked.

"That's right, Otto. Giving to others brings out the Christmas spirit in everyone."

"I love the Christmas spirit!" I barked.

"Me too, Otto! Merry Christmas!"

"Merry Christmas! *Ruff Ruff!*"

We Love Our History

Christmas: The day Christians celebrate the birth of Jesus. On this day, people enjoy traditions, sing carols, and exchange gifts with their families and friends.

Holy Land: The area in the Middle East where many important events in Jewish, Christian, and Muslim history occurred. Jesus, a Jew, lived his entire life in the area.

Three wise men: Three individuals, sometimes called "the Magi," who Christians believe traveled very far to worship Jesus when he was born. Some believe their names were Melchior, Gaspar, and Balthazar.

Gold, frankincense, and myrrh: The gifts that the three wise men gave to Jesus. Gold is a precious metal that is used to make jewelry and money. Frankincense and myrrh are substances from trees that release a pleasing scent when burned as incense. They are often used in religious ceremonies.

Jesus: A religious leader from the Holy Land in the first century who Christians regard as the Son of God and Savior of all who believe in Him. Although He was, at first, a carpenter from Nazareth, He began preaching about God's kingdom. According to Christian belief, He was crucified for the sins of humanity, and, three days later, rose from the dead, thereby conquering death.

Saint Nicholas: A Christian bishop from Greece who lived in modern-day Turkey from 270 AD-343 AD. Legend has it that he would anonymously throw bags of gold coins into the windows of the poor. The coins supposedly landed in the shoes or stockings that were drying by the fireplace, giving rise to the Christmas tradition of the "stocking stuffer." After Nicholas died and was declared a saint, his popularity and positive Christmas message spread across Europe. Some believe he is Santa Claus.

John F. Kennedy: The 35th President of the United States, from 1961-1963. He was the youngest man ever elected president and was very popular.

Jackie: Jaqueline Kennedy was the wife of John F. Kennedy and First Lady of the United States. She began the tradition of selecting a theme for the official White House Christmas tree in the Blue Room in 1961.

Irving Berlin: A Jewish American composer and songwriter who wrote many famous songs for musicals and movies during the early ragtime and jazz periods. Two of his most famous songs are "White Christmas" and "God Bless America."

PragerU Needs Your Help

You can help keep PragerU videos free and our kids books available at a low cost by making a donation at:

PragerU.com/SupportBooks

Learn more about PragerU's K-12th grade educational initiative at:

PragerU.com/Kids

About *Otto's Tales*

The Otto's Tales children's book series features young Dennis and his beloved bulldog, Otto, in thrilling adventures that educate children about America's history. Created for young readers, the Otto's Tales series is a fun, meaningful, and easy way to bring your family closer together, while passing on the values and lessons that make America so prosperous and free. Celebrate America with your children as they learn about our nation's true past, take pride in America's glorious history, and carry our shared values into the future.

Collect other books in the Otto's Tales series and learn about American holidays and traditional values in fun, imaginary tales:

- Martin Luther King, Jr. Day: A colorblind nation where everyone is created equal in God's image
- Presidents' Day: Freedom, American Exceptionalism, Nationalism
- American Trinity: Liberty, In God We Trust, E Pluribus Unum
- Mothers Day: Traditional role of mothers in the home
- Fathers Day: The importance of fathers
- Flag Day: Heritage, Honor, Pride
- Independence Day: Bravery and Liberty
- The National Anthem & Pledge of Allegiance: Patriotism, Tradition, God
- September 11th (Patriot Day): Heroism, Strength, Unity
- Columbus Day: Curiosity, Determination, Perseverance
- Veterans Day: Respect, Gratitude, Nationalism, Reverence, Remembrance
- Thanksgiving: Gratitude, Generosity, Family
- Christmas: God, Family, and Faith